W9-BXW-115

3-D ADVENTURES
DEADLY DINOSAURS

ARCTURUS

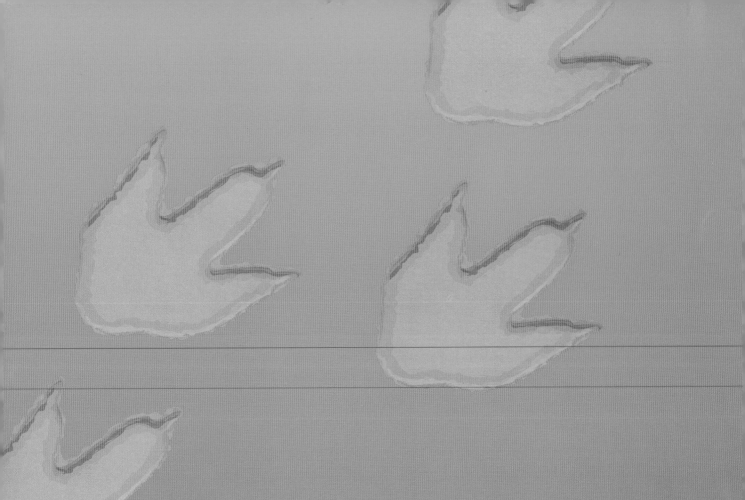

This edition published in 2011 by Arcturus Publishing Limited
26/27 Bickels Yard, 151–153 Bermondsey Street,
London SE1 3HA

Copyright © 2011 Arcturus Publishing Limited

All rights reserved. No part of this publication may be reproduced,
stored in a retrieval system, or transmitted, in any form or by any
means, electronic, mechanical, photocopying, recording or otherwise,
without written permission in accordance with the provisions of the
Copyright Act 1956 (as amended). Any person or persons who do
any unauthorised act in relation to this publication may be liable to
criminal prosecution and civil claims for damages.

ISBN: 978-1-84858-055-8
CH001938EN

Printed in China

CONTENTS

DINOSAURS: THE BASICS

A LONG REIGN

Millions and millions of years before any people lived on Earth, the world belonged to the dinosaurs. These amazing creatures first appeared about 228 million years ago. The magnificent beasts ranged in size from the knee-high to the sky-high, and ruled the Earth for about 160 million years. Humans have only been around for about 1.5 million years, so we have quite a lot of catching up to do!

DINOSAUR DAYS

Dinosaurs lived during the Mesozoic era, which began 245 million years ago and ended 65 million years ago. Each of three periods in the Mesozoic era had its own cool creatures. The Triassic period (248–206 million years ago) gave us the earliest dinosaurs, like *Herrerasaurus* (eh-ray-rah-SORE-us), as well as the first small mammals. The Jurassic period (206–142 million years ago) produced plant-eaters like *Stegosaurus* (steg-oh-SORE-us) and meat-eaters like *Allosaurus* (al-oh-SORE-us). And the Cretaceous period (142–65 million years ago) was the time of *Iguanodon* (ig-WHA-noh-don) and *Deinonychus* (die-NON-i-kus) and, sadly, it was also the end of the line for the dinosaurs.

◄ EMPTY NESTERS

Like most reptiles, dinosaurs hatched from eggs. For many years, paleontologists (scientists who study prehistoric life) thought that dinosaurs were pretty relaxed parents: in their tough neighborhood, self-preservation was a higher priority than taking care of the children! But fossils now indicate that some dinosaurs may have been very protective of their young, like one Cretaceous plant-eater who apparently guarded its babies and brought them food. This dinosaur has been named *Maiasaura* (my-ah-SORE-ah), or "good mother lizard."

▲ CAN YOU DIG IT?

When most dinosaurs died, their bodies just rotted away and nothing remained of them. But if a dinosaur died and the conditions were right, the bones would gradually become petrified (turned to stone). From these ancient remains, called fossils, paleontologists can learn what a dinosaur looked like, how it moved, and what—or who!—it ate for dinner.

Scientists believe that there are hundreds of dinosaur species yet to be found. You might make the next big discovery!

CARNIVORES

Carnivorous (meat-eating) dinosaurs wouldn't have won any popularity contests. Imagine bumping into one on a dark night! Some of them, such as the recently discovered *Giganotosaurus* (JI-gah-NO-tuh-SORE-us), were humongous, but there were also mini meat-munchers, such as *Compsognathus* (komp-soh-NAY-thus), who was no bigger than a chicken. Apart from size, these dinos had a lot of things in common, not least their liking for meat and the daggerlike claws and teeth with which to get it.

Paleontologists can learn what dinosaurs ate by examining fossils called coprolites—the scientific name for dino dung.

◄ RUN FOR YOUR LIFE!

Some of the most dangerous carnivorous dinosaurs were small but speedy—and well-armed! Deinonychus was only 12 feet long, but fast and fierce. Its name, meaning "terrible claw," refers to the long, curved claw on each of its back feet, which it used to slash its prey. It also had a relatively big brain—bad news for its intended victims.

FOOD FIGHTS ▶

While some herbivorous (plant-eating) dinosaurs may have been gentle, they didn't necessarily give up without a struggle. In Mongolia's Gobi Desert, the bones of a meat-eating *Velociraptor* (vel-O-si-RAP-tor, meaning "speedy robber") and the bones of a plant-eating *Protoceratops* (pro-toe-SER-a-tops) were found together, indicating a fight to the finish—for both of them. So much for fast food!

▼ ARMED AND DANGEROUS

At around 39 feet long, Allosaurus was the top predator of the Jurassic period. It had a powerful tail, three strong claws on each hand, and a mouthful of teeth with jagged edges, perfect for tearing and chewing flesh. You wouldn't hear this diner complain that his meat was too tough!

The huge meat-eater Megalosaurus (MEG-ah-loh-SORE-us), or "great reptile," was the first dinosaur ever to be named. When its leg bone was unearthed in 1676, people thought they had discovered the remains of a giant man.

HERBIVORES

The biggest creatures that have ever walked the Earth were the herbivorous (plant-eating) dinosaurs. Just the neck of *Mamenchisaurus* (mah-MEN-chee-SORE-us) measured 39 feet long—the length of a bus. Another long-neck, *Seismosaurus* (SIZE-moh-sore-us), may have measured around 115 feet. That's the length of two bowling alley lanes! The plant-eaters went looking for food, not trouble, so other dinosaurs had little to fear from them. But a meat-eater that provoked or attacked them might get more than it bargained for.

▲ VEGETARIAN VENGEANCE

Imagine long-necked reptiles the height of six men standing on each other's shoulders and as heavy as a dozen elephants! *Brachiosaurus* (brak-ee-oh-SORE-us) was way too massive to move fast. But it had a thick and powerful tail, great for whacking Jurassic attackers like Allosaurus and *Ceratosaurus* (seh-rat-oh-SORE-us). And while its thick, tree-like limbs weren't built for speed, Brachiosaurus might have been able to rear back on its hind legs and crash its front ones down on its enemy. Take that!

◀ TOUGH LOVE

The plant-eating *Pachycephalosaurus* (PAK-ee-SEF-a-loh-SORE-us) was a real bonehead! The solid dome on the top of its skull was 10 inches thick. Some scientists believe that during the mating season, rival males would fight for females by charging at each other headfirst. Those built-in crash helmets certainly came in handy!

▼ WEAPONS OR WEATHERPROOFING?

The strange-looking Stegosaurus, one of the most recognizable dinosaurs, has long puzzled paleontologists. Most now agree that the row of triangular plates down its back served as a sort of prehistoric furnace and air-conditioner. If Stegosaurus wanted to warm up, it stood with its side to the sun, warming the blood in the plates as it passed through on its journey around the dino's body. On a hot day, a breeze blowing through the plates would cool the Stegosaurus down.

Poor Stegosaurus has another claim to fame besides its weird appearance: its walnut-sized brain was smaller than any other dinosaur's.

The polished pebbles found among some plant-eating dinosaur remains suggest that before they gulped down their leafy lunches, some dinosaurs may have swallowed stones to help grind up their food.

DINO KING?

When you hear the word "dinosaur," it is probably T. rex that comes to mind first. *Tyrannosaurus rex* (tie-RAN-oh-SORE-us REX), whose name means "king of the tyrant lizards," is so notorious that we have dedicated a whole chapter to it later in this book. One of the biggest, fiercest meat-eating dinosaurs, T. rex had huge, powerful jaws—and an appetite to match! Amazingly, in 1993, a carnivorous dinosaur was unearthed that was even bigger and fiercer than T. rex. Giganotosaurus may be the biggest meat-eating dinosaur discovered to date, but the king will always loom large in every dino fan's imagination.

▶ TYRANT OR TRASH CAN?

T. rex certainly had the equipment of a killing machine. But some scientists argue that with its huge bulk and short arms, which were probably useless for catching prey, Tyrannosaurus rex was probably not the most efficient of hunters. It may have obtained most of its food by feeding on sick or wounded prey—or even by eating the leftovers of other carnivores.

A single T. rex would have eaten the equivalent of about 290 people a year!

▲ ALL THE BETTER TO EAT YOU WITH

Tyrannosaurus rex was certainly a bigmouth! With a head as long as a refrigerator, it could have opened its jaws wide enough to swallow a man in one gulp. Curved, jagged teeth, longer than a human hand, could puncture its prey's organs before tearing it apart. T. rex's teeth were made for ripping, not chewing, so it had to swallow each mouthful whole. What dreadful table manners!

SUPER-REX

In 1990, one of the largest and most complete Tyrannosaurus skeletons ever unearthed was found in South Dakota. Named "Sue," after its discoverer, this fossilized dinosaur was a real tough customer. A number of its bones had been broken but had rehealed over time. The broken bones were probably a result of fierce battles with other T. rex.

THE RIGHTFUL KING ▶

Giganotosaurus, whose name means "giant lizard of the south," was discovered in Argentina in 1993. When this dinosaur's skull and thighbone were found to be bigger than Sue's, it became clear that Tyrannosaurus was rex no more! How long will Giganotosaurus be number 1? Its reign could end at any time, since new types of dinosaurs are being found every year. But until then—long live the (new) king!

SWIMMERS

hile dinosaurs roamed the Earth, equally awesome beasts ruled the seas. Many of these oceanic monsters evolved from land reptiles and adapted to life in the water. But though some looked pretty fishy, they were still reptiles, and had to come to the surface to breathe between dives, just like whales and dolphins. The prehistoric sea monsters came in all shapes and sizes. Some had long necks and flippers, while others had long jaws filled with razor-sharp teeth. One of the biggest, *Kronosaurus* (KRON-oh-SORE-us), with its huge 8-foot head, feasted on prehistoric squid, sharks—and its fellow seafaring reptiles!

Beautifully preserved fossils suggest that Ichthyosaurs didn't lay eggs but gave birth to their little ones live in the water.

▼ A SPOT OF FISHING

Ichthyosaurs (IKH-thee-oh-sores), like this 50-foot-long *Shonisaurus* (shon-ee-SORE-us), were the super swimmers of the prehistoric seas. They looked a lot like modern-day dolphins—but they were much, much bigger. With sleek bodies, back fins, and strong tails, Ichthyosaurs zipped through the water as fast as 25 miles per hour. When their big eyes spotted a tasty meal, their long, tooth-lined jaws would open and snap! Fish *du jour*!

◀ MONSTER OR MYTH?

Sea monster sightings have been reported all over the world. The most famous of these creatures is Scotland's "Nessie," the so-called Loch Ness Monster. Descriptions of Nessie—and a photo that turned out to be a fake—suggested that it could have been a Plesiosaur. Few people today believe monsters like Nessie exist... but you never know!

DOWN IN THE DEPTHS ▶

With their skinny necks and roly-poly bodies, *Plesiosaurs* (PLE-see-oh-sores) may have looked awkward, but thanks to paddle-like flippers that let them twist and turn, they were able to swim at high speeds to catch food with their sharp teeth. To help them sink when they wanted to stay below the surface, they sometimes swallowed rocks to act as ballast. Now there's an appetizer that would fill anyone up!

FLIERS

n prehistoric times, reptiles not only ruled the Earth and seas but also filled the skies. The *Pterosaurs* (TEH-ruh-sores) were flying reptiles with wings made of skin. They fed on creatures from both land and sea. Some Pterosaurs were tiny; others had a wingspan equivalent to that of a small airplane—along with knife-sharp teeth. Look out below!

Quetzalcoatlus (kwet-zal-co-AT-lus) was the largest creature ever to sail the skies. And sail or glide on air currents is what it probably did; its enormous wings may have been too big to flap!

▼ SUPER SCOOPER

Pteranodon (Ter-RAN-oh-don) was one funny-looking fisherman. Its head had a pointy crest and even pointier jaws. Pteranodon would skim through the water, scoop up fish, and swallow them whole—the same handy method used by pelicans today.

AIR-VOLUTION ▶

Rhamphorynchus (RAM-foh-RING-khus), one of the early Pterosaurs, had spiky teeth, great for spearing fish. It also had a long, kite-like tail that may have helped it steer through the skies. Later flying reptiles like Quetzalcoatlus looked quite different, with much shorter tails but longer necks.

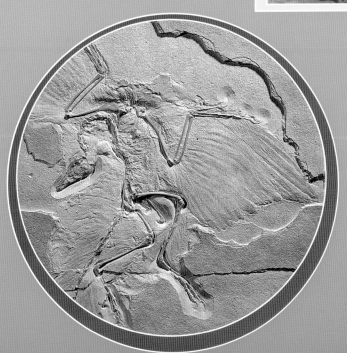

◀ FINALLY...FEATHERS!

Archaeopteryx (ark-ee-OP-ter-iks), which means "ancient wing," is the first flying reptile known to have had feathery wings. But don't let the feathers fool you—this was no ordinary bird. Its fossils reveal the skeleton of a reptile with dinosaur-like teeth and claws on its wings, which it may have used to climb trees. Some scientists think it may have been more of a glider than a flier—okay at catching a breeze, but lousy at take-offs!

DINO DEMISE

Around 65 million years ago the dinosaurs disappeared from the face of the planet. There are lots of different theories about why this happened, but for many years most people believed the reason the dinosaurs died out was that a large asteroid hit the Earth. The clouds of rubble, dust, and other debris that the impact threw up blocked out the Sun's rays, and this in turn made temperatures drop. The dinosaurs couldn't cope with the colder weather and died off. But is this what *really* happened?

▼ THERE GOES THE NEIGHBORHOOD

It would take a massive asteroid to alter the planet like this and it would leave a mighty big hole. And such a hole exists—it's called the Chicxulub crater and it's off the Yucatán Peninsula of Mexico. Most of the crater is covered by the sea, but we now know it is over 111 miles across. That's one big hole!

CROSSING THE BOUNDARY

To make a hole as big as Chicxulub, the asteroid would have been about 6 miles across. Debris thrown up by the impact of this asteroid has been found all round the world and can be seen as a layer in the rocks, which paleontologists call the K/T boundary. There are dinosaur fossils below this layer but none above it.

DISPROVED ▶

Some people claim that mammals may have eaten all the dinosaur eggs, but that's a lot of eggs for the tiny mammals of the time to have consumed. Other theories about the demise of the dinos include a lack of vegetation for the plant-eating dinosaurs to munch on—if the plant-eaters had died out, then so would the carnivorous dinosaurs who preyed on them. Another theory is that exploding stars killed the dinosaurs with radiation. None of these theories really fits the bill, however.

◀ GRADUAL DECLINE

A large number of paleontologists point out that dinosaurs were on the decline for millions of years and the climate was changing, partly due to an increase in volcanic eruptions. No doubt an asteroid strike would have speeded up the rate at which the dinosaurs disappeared, but if the climate was changing anyway, the dinosaurs' time was limited.

Another interesting question—why did dinosaurs disappear and other animals, such as mammals, survive?

DINOSAURS: THE FACTS

DINO DETAILS

S o we know when and for how long dinosaurs ruled our planet before disappearing under mysterious circumstances. Now it's time to find out exactly what these amazing creatures were like. Get ready for an up-close meeting!

◄ STAND UP STRAIGHT

Dinosaurs were a type of reptile, but they were very different from other reptiles, such as lizards or crocodiles. In fact, they were so different that the dinosaurs' closest living relatives today are actually birds. The most obvious difference between reptiles and dinosaurs is the way they stood. Dinosaurs' legs were underneath their bodies, like a modern-day cow or lion, not to the side like other reptiles.

▲ DINO BABIES

Like reptiles and birds, dinosaurs laid eggs. Nest sites have been found all over the world and it would appear that many types of dinosaur took care of their young, possibly in much the same way as crocodiles do today. Herding dinosaurs like Maiasaura—the "good mother lizard"—would nest together in large areas called nesting sites.

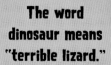

The word dinosaur means "terrible lizard."

▶ NOT A DINOSAUR

The dinosaurs shared the planet with lots of other animals such as insects, fish, and even some small mammals. There were also some flying reptiles including *Pterodactyls* (teh-roh-DAK-til), and ones that swam, such as Ichthyosaurs (below). Although many people often call these creatures dinosaurs, they are wrong. Dinosaurs lived only on the land, not in the air or underwater.

DINO LIFE

There have been hundreds of different species of dinosaur discovered so far. Their remains show that many of them developed some interesting features to help them in their daily lives.

▼ CLOSE COMMUNICATION

Some members of the hadrosaur family, such as *Parasaurolophus* (pa-rah-sore-row-LOFF-us), had a large crest on their heads. The crest had tubes in it, which flowed all the way down the dinosaur's snout. This allowed Parasaurolophus to blow air through them—a bit like a musician blowing into a trumpet. Scientists believe that Parasaurolophus used this noise as a means of communicating with other members of its herd.

▶ THE FEATHERS FLY

The discovery of Archaeopteryx shed a whole new light on dinosaurs as it was clear that some of them had feathers. The question is, how many had them? Feathers are so delicate they are not often preserved as fossils, so it is difficult to know for sure. Now scientists think that many of the smaller dinosaurs might have been completely feathered too.

◀ DEADLY CLAW

The raptors, such as *Utahraptor* (YOU-tah-RAP-tore), were not the biggest carnivorous dinosaurs, but they did have an especially deadly weapon. Raptors had a large claw on each foot that swiveled. When they pounced on their victims, their claws would come stabbing down in a deadly arc that would puncture the main blood vessels or air tubes of their prey.

ARMOR-PLATED

With so many meat-eaters about, it made sense to be as well protected as possible. Possibly the most heavily protected was *Ankylosaurus* (an-kee-loh-SORE-us). Its skin was covered with thick plates of bone, so it looked like it was wearing a suit of armor. If all that wasn't enough, Ankylosaurus also had large bony lumps at the end of its tail, which it would swing like a club.

The next time you see a bird, think of how it is descended from a dinosaur. It's an awesome concept!

EARLY DINOS

The time when dinosaurs were alive has been split into three different periods, each markedly different from the other and each with its own distinct types of dinosaur. The first is called the Triassic period, which lasted from 248 to 206 million years ago. The dinosaurs were not around at the start of this period and had only evolved by the end of it.

OLDEST FIND

Possibly the oldest dinosaur fossil discovered so far belongs to a small dinosaur called *Eoraptor* (ee-oh-RAP-tore), which means "dawn thief." It was about 3 feet long and dates from around 228 million years ago. Like all of the earliest dinosaurs, Eoraptor walked on two legs and was a meat-eater.

Some scientists think Eoraptor isn't a dinosaur at all but a dino ancestor.

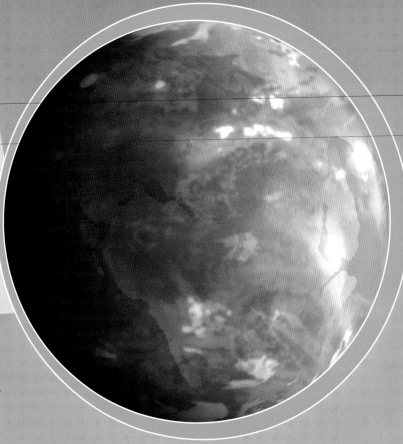

▲ SAME WORLD, DIFFERENT LOOK

The planet looked a lot different at the start of the Triassic period compared to today. Instead of all the different continents as we know them, there was just one large landmass, which scientists call a supercontinent. They named this supercontinent Pangaea and, during the course of the Triassic, it slowly began to break apart. Conditions on Pangaea were very dry, but the weather was warm—ideal for reptiles like the dinosaurs to flourish, as many scientists believe that they needed heat to warm their bodies before they could move quickly.

▼ PREHISTORIC FLIPPER

A Plesiosaur was an aquatic reptile that evolved along with the dinosaurs about 220 million years ago, toward the end of the Triassic period. It had a broad body with four large flippers and a fairly short tail. Some Plesiosaurs were less than 7 feet long. A Plesiosaur had a very small head at the end of a very long neck, which made it look as though its head was on the end of its tail! By contrast, its larger cousin the Pliosaur—up to 65 feet long—had a large head and short neck.

▲ GREEN ISSUES

Most of the plants that we know today would not have been present during the Triassic period. Perhaps the most noticeable difference was that there was no grass—in fact, no dinosaur would ever have seen grass. There were no flowering plants either, just plants with lots of leaves.

JURASSIC PARK

After the Triassic period came the Jurassic period, also called "the age of reptiles." This period lasted from 206 to around 144 million years ago. Some of the most well-known and largest of all the dinosaurs lived during the Jurassic period.

Some sauropods had longer front legs than back legs. This meant they could reach leaves at the top of the tallest trees.

▼ THE GIANTS

The Jurassic period was the time of the giant sauropod dinosaurs. The sauropods walked on four thick, stout legs and had long necks and tails. The front legs of some sauropods were shorter than their back legs, which meant that their necks pointed downwards. This tells scientists that they fed on vegetation growing close to the ground. The great size and whiplike tail of *Diplodocus* (DIP-loh-doh-cus) was enough to dissuade even the fiercest meat-eater from attacking it.

▲ ALL CHANGE

During the Jurassic period, Pangaea began to break up into two supercontinents called Laurasia and Gondwana and as a result the climate became much wetter than in the Triassic period. Laurasia was in the Northern Hemisphere and Gondwana in the Southern.

◀ CURIOUS PLATES

Scientists have concluded that the plates on a Stegosaurus's back were to help the dinosaur control its temperature, but it was once thought that they were to discourage predators from a tempting Stegosaurus snack. However, further study has revealed that the plates weren't really too sturdy, although the 3-foot-long, spearlike spikes on its tail would have been excellent weapons.

▼ LEADER OF THE PACK

One of the most common of the meat-eating dinosaurs was Allosaurus. Around 39 feet in length, Allosaurus was a fearsome sight. Scientists believe that Allosaurus may well have been a pack hunter, a bit like a modern-day lion. Hunting in packs suggests a degree of intelligence, as teamwork involves cooperation and tactics.

FINAL DINOS

The Cretaceous period marked the end of the reign of the dinosaurs. When the last of them died out around 65 million years ago, it paved the way for the animal world to become more diverse and numerous.

THE GREAT KING

One of the last dinosaurs to evolve—and probably the most famous of all—was Tyrannosaurus rex, one of the biggest and heaviest carnivorous dinosaurs. With its long, serrated teeth and excellent senses of smell and sight, it was a truly terrifying prospect for unwary plant-eaters. Its massive skull was balanced by a long, heavy tail.

▼ PRINCE ALBERT

T. rex had some smaller cousins, like *Albertosaurus* (al-bert-oh-SORE-us). Although Albertosaurus lacked its famous relative's size, it made up for it in a different way. The discovery of a number of Albertosaurus remains in 1910 indicated that these 30-foot-long dinosaurs lived and hunted in packs. If a victim escaped one Albertosaurus, there was always another to take up the hunt.

Did you know that many species of reptiles, fish, insects, and mammals also disappeared around the same time as the dinosaurs?

▲ FLOWERY DELIGHTS

By the end of the Cretaceous period, the supercontinents had broken up and the resulting smaller continents began to look a little more as they do today. The vegetation also started to look more familiar, as trees and flowering plants such as magnolia appeared. The climate was warm too, and by the end of the period there was increased volcanic activity—which may have led to the dinosaurs' extinction.

◄ HERDS OF HORNS

Another of the last dinosaur species was the plant-eating *Triceratops* (tri-SEH-ra-tops), which lived in herds. A large group of angry Triceratops was much more difficult to attack than a single animal, so herd living clearly had its advantages. Some scientists believe that when Triceratops came under attack, they would stand in a circle facing outward with the young Triceratops hiding in the center. A predator would think twice before attacking such a lineup!

ALL SIZES

Dinosaurs came in small, medium, large, and super size! There was a size and shape of dinosaur to fit every situation. It's not easy to say which were the true record holders as so many dinosaur fossils are incomplete, leaving room for much speculation.

▶ LONGEST

The longest dinosaur discovered so far is called Seismosaurus. This giant was part of the Diplodocus family and stretched up to 115 feet long. Like Diplodocus, much of the length of Seismosaurus was made up by its neck and tail. Despite its length, Seismosaurus wasn't a very tall dinosaur. At only 16 feet high, it was a third of the size of giants such as Brachiosaurus.

▲ MOST EXPENSIVE

Well-preserved and near-complete dinosaur fossils are rare and generally are not available for sale. But that's exactly what happened when a Tyrannosaurus rex fossil was auctioned in 1997. It was nicknamed "Sue" after Sue Hendrickson, the scientist who found it, and it became the most famous fossil on the planet. When it sold for a staggering $8.4 million, it also became the most expensive. Fortunately for the general public, a museum and not a wealthy private collector bought it. So now anyone can see Sue at the Field Museum in Chicago.

New dinosaurs are being discovered all the time, particularly in China. So who knows how long these records will last!

SMALLEST

Possibly the smallest dinosaur of all was *Microraptor* (my-crow-RAP-tore). This bird-sized dinosaur was discovered in China in 2001. Its size isn't the only thing that made it special—it also had wings. Some scientists believe that it wasn't capable of flying, but could glide from tree to tree instead. Microraptor may have evolved wings to avoid predators.

▶ TALLEST

The tallest dinosaur comes from the Jurassic period. Unsurprisingly, it was one of the giant sauropods, Brachiosaurus. It stood around 50 feet high—about nine times taller than a human being.

REAL OR NOT?

The story of dinosaur discovery is littered with tales of mistaken identity, incorrect suppositions, and downright lies. Generally the mistakes are uncovered over time when further discoveries are made, but who knows how much of what we know today will prove to be as incorrect as these examples?

▼ ALREADY DISCOVERED

Many dinosaur species are known only from small fragments of bone, so it's easy to see how mistakes can be made. This is exactly what happened in the case of a once well-known dinosaur called *Brontosaurus* (bron-toh-SORE-us). Although the remains were quite complete, they turned out to be the same as a dinosaur called *Apatosaurus* (a-pat-oh-SORE-us), a giant that weighed as much as four elephants. Apatosaurus means "deceptive lizard," which proved to be a very appropriate name!

EARLY ERROR

When the remains of Iguanodon were found in the 1880s, it was only the second type of dinosaur to be discovered. The remains were incomplete and the scientists reconstructed it as a heavy, stocky-looking creature with a horn on its nose. The "horn" was really one of Iguanodon's thumb spikes!

Fossil remains are big business, so be careful. There are a lot of fakes out there!

FAKE FIND

Lots of exciting fossils have come from China in recent years. In 1999 it was thought the fossil that finally proved birds were descended from dinosaurs had been found there. The discovery of the dinosaur called *Archeoraptor* received worldwide attention—and so did the realization that it was a fake. It was really a couple of different fossils stuck together in an attempt to make it more valuable to collectors.

▼ WHAT'S IN A NAME?

Gryposaurus (GRIP-oh-SAUR-us), a duck-billed dinosaur found in North America in the late Cretaceous period, was around 33 feet long and weighed up to 2 tons. The large bump on its snout made it look fearsome, but this plant-eater was quite peaceful. It was once thought to be closely related to *Kritosaurus* (KRIT-oh-SAUR-us), and they even shared a name for a time—Gryposaurus was also known as *Kritosaurus notabilis*—but scientists now think Kritosaurus is a separate genus.

HEAD BANGERS ▶

When the strange dome-shaped skull of *Pachycephalosaurus* (pak-ee-SEF-a-loh-SORE-us) was discovered, it was thought the dinosaur used it to headbutt rival males in the way some rams do today. However, research now shows that the skulls just weren't strong enough for this kind of behavior. Why the skulls were shaped like that still remains a mystery.

T. REX

THE KING

The magnificent creatures known as dinosaurs came in all shapes and sizes but, as we have already discovered, one in particular stands out from all the rest—the world's most famous dinosaur species, Tyrannosaurus rex. But what was this regal dinosaur really like? Was it as fearsome as it first appears? What food did it eat? How fast could it run? What color was it? How did it raise its young? These are all questions scientists are still trying to answer to this day.

◄ BIG BOY

Tyrannosaurus rex was the largest of the Tyrannosaur family of dinosaurs that lived in North America around 85 to 65 million years ago. Tyrannosaurus rex was also one of the biggest carnivorous, or meat-eating, dinosaurs ever discovered. It measured over 40 feet from nose to tail, and was around 13 feet tall at the hips. It weighed between 6 and 8 tons, too, which means it was heavier than an elephant and longer than two small trucks.

► CHANGING WORLD

The Cretaceous world was very different from the one we know today. The landmasses were still in motion and even the shape of the continents was different. By the time T. rex appeared, however, the two large supercontinents of Gondawana and Laurasia had broken apart and started to form the continents that we know today.

It is thought that female Tyrannosaurs were bigger than their male counterparts.

END OF AN ERA

The period of history when the dinosaurs were alive is called the Mesozoic era. The same types of dinosaur weren't alive for all of this time. Tyrannosaurus rex was alive during the Cretaceous period, at the end of the reign of the dinosaurs.

KEEP OFF THE GRASS ►

On the land things were pretty different, too. The closest you would get to mammals like us were four-legged, furry creatures, most no bigger than a mouse. You might recognize some of the vegetation. There were ferns, and trees such as conifers, ginkgos, and sycamores, but as we know, there were no grasses. At least you didn't have to worry about T. rex ruining your lawn!

39

AMAZING FIND

There have been around thirty T. rex skeletons discovered so far, but not all of these are in good condition and many are far from complete. A good specimen therefore attracts a lot of attention—sometimes a little bit *too* much attention in the case of the Field Museum of Chicago's prize exhibit.

▲ FEMME FATALE

Sue, the most famous Tyrannosaurus rex of all, can be found at the Field Museum in Chicago. She is one of the most complete skeletons of a T. rex found to date, and also the largest. The skeleton is so well preserved that it has helped paleontologists to learn a great deal more about these magnificent dinosaurs.

SIOUX SUE OVER SUE

Sue was discovered in 1990 near Faith in South Dakota, by a team from the Black Hills Institute. A huge row soon erupted over who actually owned the skeleton. There were four claims: the first by the team that found her; the second by the Sioux Indians on whose reservation she had been found; the third by the man who owned the ranch where Sue was found; and the fourth by the government. After many years of legal battles, Sue was awarded to the rancher who auctioned her in 1997 for a gigantic sum.

▲ NUMBER ONE

The first Tyrannosaurus rex found was discovered in 1902 by a fossil hunter called Barnum Brown. Today, scientists like Jack Horner (above) are continuing his work.

Sue's skeleton was so complete it even included a wishbone (furcula).

STAN THE MAN

The Black Hills Institute has another famous T. rex, called Stan. This skeleton was found in Hell's Creek, South Dakota, by an amateur fossil hunter called Stan Sacrison. Like Sue, Stan the dino had suffered some injuries in his life, such as broken bones—probably from fights with other Tyrannosaurs! Do you think there's a chance that Sue and Stan met?

▶ MOVING MONSTER

Improvements in robotic engineering mean that moving, or animatronic, models can bring prehistoric creatures to life. Visitors to museums such as London's Natural History Museum can get within touching distance of a ferocious roaring Tyrannosaur—luckily this is as close as anyone will ever get to being face-to-face with a T. rex.

DEATH TRAP!

Without a doubt, it's the Tyrannosaur's fearsome head that makes it such a scary and impressive dinosaur. At around 5 feet long, its skull was as big as a twelve-year-old child and packed with dangerous-looking teeth. This was the business end of the T. rex, and other dinosaurs were well advised to keep clear of it!

Tyrannosaurs were always growing new teeth, so when an old one fell out or got knocked out, a new one was ready to replace it.

MOUTHFUL OF MISERY

If you were unfortunate enough to see inside a Tyrannosaur's mouth, you'd see up to sixty good reasons to want to be somewhere else. That's the number of razor-sharp teeth a Tyrannosaur had. The teeth could measure up to 6 inches in length and they curved backward. This peculiar shape meant that when a Tyrannosaur bit anything, it was one mouthful that wouldn't get away.

◀ BIG BITE

Scientists have figured out that a T. rex could easily chomp its way through thick dinosaur bones. Anything unlucky enough to get in its way would be lucky to survive.

▼ SMALL ARMS

Another big question—what were the T. rex's arms for? They were so small they couldn't reach the Tyrannosaur's mouth, and would have been useless for picking things up as they only had two claws at the end. However, these claws were really sharp and paleontologists have determined that the arms were very strong—a puzzling, if short, mystery.

MEET THE NEIGHBORS

As big and fearsome as Tyrannosaurus rex was, unbelievably it may not have been the largest meat-eating dinosaur of the Cretaceous period. Giganotosaurus from Argentina and *Carcharodontosaurus* (car-CHA-row-DON-toe-SORE-us) from Morocco might well have been bigger. However, T. rex appears to have been heavier than both of these giant meat-eaters, so it remains the true heavyweight carnivore champ.

FOOD FACTS

Everyone agrees that Tyrannosaurs were the super-carnivores of their time. But what paleontologists can't agree on is whether this fearsome-looking dinosaur hunted for its food or was a scavenger. Animals that scavenge search out and eat other animals who have died or already been killed, instead of hunting live prey. The hunter or scavenger question is still a hot topic among the experts, and shows no sign of being resolved at any time in the near future.

▲ HEADSTRONG

If T. rex was a scavenger, why did it have such a strong head? The skull bones are really tough and could easily handle a strong impact, such as the sort you would expect if it were attacking another dinosaur.

◄ BIG NOSE

Paleontologists who argue that T. rex was a scavenger point to its keen sense of smell. It's true that scavengers, such as vultures, can smell rotting meat from a great distance, but maybe T. rex was a hunter who used its sense of smell to track its prey.

SLOWPOKE

One thing's for sure, Tyrannosaurus rex was no speed freak. After studying the dinosaur's leg bones and muscles, scientists believe Tyrannosaurs had a top speed of about 25 miles per hour—faster than a human, but pretty slow when compared to many dinosaurs. Worse still, it seems that T. rex could only keep up this speed for short bursts.

▶ EYE CAN SEE YOU

One of the strongest arguments in favor of Tyrannosaurus being a hunter rather than a scavenger is the position of its eyes. The eyes face forward, like a human's, rather than to the side, like a horse. Forward-facing eyes give a better sense of exactly where objects are, which is why top predators such as tigers have eyes in this position. Mind you, so do some scavengers, such as hyenas.

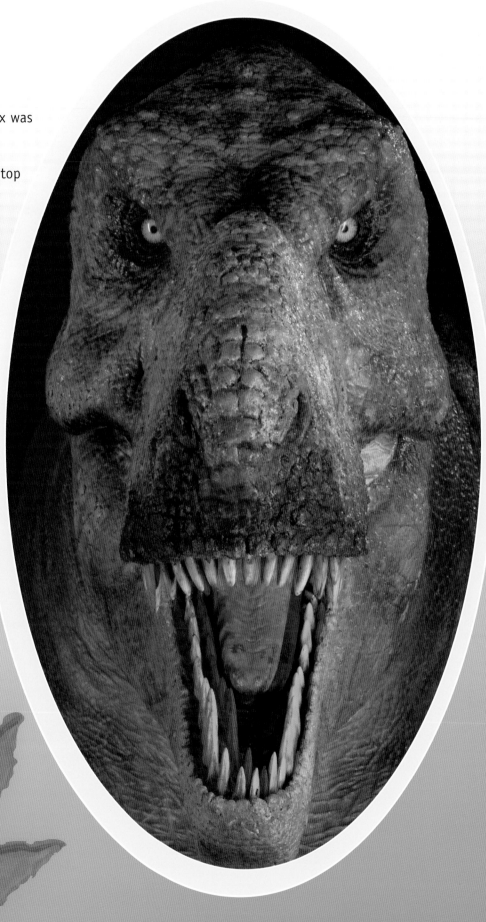

As T. rex hunted in dense forests, perhaps speed was not so important.

EARLY LIFE

What was life like for a baby Tyrannosaur? Certainly the Cretaceous forest was a dangerous place for a juvenile. It could be crushed by large plant-eating dinosaurs or eaten by other carnivores. There was even a possibility that the young Tyrannosaur could get eaten by one of its parents. Life was certainly tough for Cretaceous kids!

◄ HATCHING OUT

Like all dinosaurs, Tyrannosaurus would have started life in an egg. So far, no Tyrannosaur eggs have been discovered, so we can't be sure what they looked like. Some paleontologists think the most likely shape for the eggs would have been long and thin. The eggs would probably have been laid in a nest, but it is unlikely that Tyrannosaurs would have sat on their nests like birds—surely they would have been too heavy? Perhaps they covered the eggs in earth or leaves, in the same way that crocodiles do today to keep their eggs warm.

FEATHERED FRIEND ▶

As we have seen, many experts believe that birds are descended from dinosaurs. Recent finds in China support this idea, as they show that some dinosaurs had feathers. It is now thought that some baby dinosaurs may have had feathers to keep them warm, too.

GROUPIES?

It's generally believed that Tyrannosaurs were solitary dinosaurs, because adult skeletons are usually found by themselves. However, nobody really knows if T. rex lived in groups or not. If they did live in a pack, it would certainly have made hunting easier for fairly slow dinosaurs like these.

A baby T. rex with feathers might have looked like a very ferocious chicken!

GOOD PARENTS

Were Tyrannosaurs good parents? Some paleontologists think that a mother Tyrannosaur, like many carnivorous predators today—such as lions—would have looked after her young, teaching them how to hunt or how to find carrion (dead animals). However, it is also thought that male Tyrannosaurs would see young Tyrannosaurs as a threat, and would try to kill and eat them. That doesn't sound like good parenting!

FOSSIL FOCUS

Everything we know about dinosaurs comes from the painstaking work of fossil hunters, paleontologists, and other scientists. We now know more than ever about dinosaurs, and the newest technology is being used to try to find out more. Fossils are scanned, magnified, and X-rayed, and computers are used to try to determine what the dinosaurs looked like and how they moved and lived. But there's still plenty we don't know.

▼ GOING UNDERGROUND

Preparing fossils is a time-consuming business. It can take paleontologists thousands of hours working on a fossil, from the moment it is discovered to the day it is shown in a museum. For example, it took years to dig up Sue's remains and prepare her for display.

▵ QUESTION OF COLOR

Fossils can tell us a great deal, but they can't tell us what color T. rex was, so paleontologists look at animals today for clues. Hunters, such as lions, aren't bright pink in color as they would be spotted a mile off. Instead they are a dull color to blend into the background. Perhaps the same was true for T. rex.

We can't tell from fossils what sort of noise T. rex made. Did it roar, or did it squeak, cluck, hiss, or bark?

▲ DIRTY BUSINESS

Being a paleontologist isn't very glamorous, especially if your job is inspecting dinosaur poo (coprolite) to discover what dinosaurs ate. From coprolites, paleontologists can tell a lot about dinosaur diets. It's a dirty job but someone's got to do it!

WARM OR COLD?

Another question puzzling paleontologists is whether T. rex was warm- or cold-blooded. Mammals like tigers, horses, and humans are warm-blooded. This means our bodies are ready to move as soon as we wake up. Reptiles are cold-blooded, which means they need to warm up in the sun before they can start moving about. However, birds, which are believed to have evolved from dinosaurs, are warm-blooded. If the dinosaurs were cold-blooded, how long do you think it would have taken a big dino like T. rex to warm up in the morning?

GIANT DINOSAURS

GIANTS RULE!

No human has ever seen a real live dinosaur, yet they are still amazingly popular. So what is it about these prehistoric creatures that keeps us so intrigued? Part of it is undoubtedly down to the incredible size of some of them. They were gigantic—the biggest animals ever to walk the Earth.

▼ KINGS OF THE WORLD

The first dinosaurs, such as Eoraptor, who appeared during the Triassic period of the Mesozoic era, were tiny. By the Jurassic period, giants such as *Camarasaurus* (kam-a-rah-SORE-us) stalked the planet.

◄ BIG IS BEST?

Although dinosaurs came in many shapes and sizes— some were as small as a crow—a surprising number of them were massive. Being big and strong meant that they were relatively safe from attack. Even ferocious meat-eaters were wary of tangling with a super-sized sauropod such as *Barosaurus* (ba-row-SORE-us). But being big wasn't always best. Giant dinosaurs needed giant meals, so if food was scarce, they could easily starve.

▶ LAND SPREAD

The remains of giant dinosaurs have been found practically everywhere on Earth. This is because they were around throughout the whole time that the original single landmass—Pangaea—was breaking apart to make the separate continents we know today.

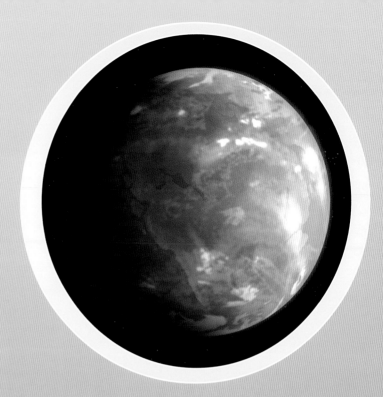

Some giant dinosaurs had nostrils on top of their heads, so people used to think they lived underwater.

▼ HIP HOORAY

Dinosaurs were reptiles, but they had legs under their bodies rather than bent out to the sides like normal reptiles (look at a crocodile to see the difference). Dinosaur hip bones differed too, and it was this difference that helped scientists link dinosaurs with their modern-day descendants: birds. Of course, the legs of gigantic dinosaurs were much bigger than those of birds—a Brachiosaurus's leg was around five times longer than the leg of an ostrich, the biggest bird alive today.

LUNCHTIME!

The popular idea of dinosaurs as gigantic, sharp-toothed monsters stomping around is actually based on fact. The dinosaur world had its fair share of huge carnivores and, for them, most of the plant-eaters out there were easy prey.

AFRICAN GIANT ▶

Carcharodontosaurus was one dinosaur to be wary of during the Cretaceous period. At around 46 feet, it was even longer than T. rex though probably not quite as bulky. Carcharodontosaurus means "shark-toothed lizard" and one look at its 6.5-foot-long skull full of sharp teeth would be enough to scare the living daylights out of most dinosaurs.

◀ GROWTH SPURT

Tyrannosaurus rex probably did most of its growing during its teenage years. From examining various T. rex remains, scientists have been able to determine that it probably gained around 1,300 pounds a year between the ages of fourteen and eighteen. It probably reached maturity at around age twenty.

SCARY SOUTHERNER ▶

South America had its own giant meat-eating menace long before T. rex terrorized North America. It is believed that Giganotosaurus was over 40 feet long and lived during the middle of the Cretaceous period. Its skull alone may have been nearly 7 feet long. Paleontologists are learning more about Giganotosaurus every day.

There were nearly twice as many plant-eating dinosaurs as meat-eating dinosaurs.

▼ TEAM LEADER

Only one thing could be more frightening than bumping into a giant meat-eating dinosaur—bumping into lots of them! Allosaurus lived in North America during the Jurassic period. At around 16 feet high it was a formidable creature, and may well have hunted in packs. Although not the biggest of the giant dinosaurs, by working as a team a pack of Allosaurus could have attacked even the biggest plant-eaters.

VAST VEGGIES

The Jurassic and Cretaceous periods saw massive herds of herbivorous (plant-eating) dinosaurs roaming the land. The long-necked sauropods, the large-frilled ceratopsids, and the bulky hadrosaurs all moved about in huge, plant-munching numbers.

SPIKY ▶

At over 30 feet long and around 7.5 tons in weight, Stegosaurus was a massive dinosaur, but it wasn't built for speed. Its main defense was its tail, which had 3-foot-long spikes—enough to make most carnivores think twice about attacking. Recently, paleontologists have taken to calling this spiky arrangement a "thagomizer," an invented word that first appeared in a comic strip in the early 1980s.

◀ DAINTY TEETH

Pachycephalosaurus lived in North America during the Cretaceous period. It could grow up to 16 feet in length and weighed a chunky 4,400 pounds. Beneath its large, dome-shaped head were two round eyes that faced forward, suggesting that it had a wide field of vision. Its teeth, however, were tiny, especially when compared with those of the carnivorous dinosaurs.

GET THE POINT ▶

One of the most famous plant-eating dinosaurs is Triceratops. Standing around 10 feet high and solidly built, the comparison with today's rhinoceros is clear. However, despite its horns Triceratops did not charge at other dinos. Recent studies show that a Triceratops risked breaking them if it hit another dinosaur at full speed. Instead, it seems that Triceratops used its horns to push or jab at a predator. Either way, the carnivore would soon have got the point!

◀ HARD-RUNNING HADROSAUR

Edmontosaurus (ed-mon-toe-SORE-us) belonged to the hadrosaur family, also known as "duck-billed" dinosaurs. These peaceful plant-eaters lived in large herds that ranged across North America during the Cretaceous period. Despite being over 40 feet long and weighing around 3.3 tons, Edmontosaurus could run as fast as a horse—which was handy for escaping a hungry meat-eater.

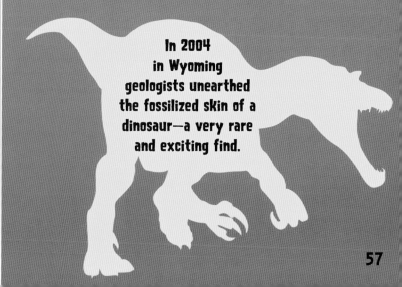

In 2004 in Wyoming geologists unearthed the fossilized skin of a dinosaur—a very rare and exciting find.

57

SAUROPODS

The biggest animals of the Mesozoic era were the sauropods—our dinosaur friends with the long necks and tails. Balancing on four stocky legs, these gentle giants lived in herds and ate enormous amounts of vegetation to fill their massive stomachs.

◀ LONG NECK, SMALL BRAIN

Diplodocus had both a long neck and tail. However, compared with its huge body, its head was very small, with space for only a small brain. Its tail contained around eighty vertebrae and probably acted as a counterbalance for the long neck.

MISTAKEN IDENTITY ▶

Not so long ago, one of the most famous of the sauropods was a species called Brontosaurus. This 80-foot-long giant was the first sauropod to be exhibited when it went on show at the American Museum of Natural History in 1905. But it was a case of mistaken identity. Brontosaurus was really Apatosaurus, who had been discovered some years previously.

▲ ARMOR-PLATED

At around 40 feet in length, *Saltasaurus* (sol-tah-SORE-us) was on the small side compared to some of the biggest sauropods. However, as its size alone was not enough to deter the carnivorous intentions of meat-eaters, it relied upon another tactic. Saltasaurus was covered in small bony plates that acted as a kind of armor, making it one tough nut to crack.

Diplodocus may have used its tail like a whip to make a loud "crack" as a warning to others.

STICK YOUR NECK OUT ▶

If sauropods were rated for their long necks, then Mamenchisaurus must rank as one of the best, as this dinosaur had the longest neck of any dinosaur. At around 39 feet in length, its neck made up nearly half of the dinosaur's 85-foot length. A neck that long would have been very handy when reaching for vegetation to eat.

UP IN THE AIR

While giant dinosaurs stalked the Earth, flying reptiles soared in the skies overhead. Some of these fascinating creatures were as small as blackbirds, but others, the largest known flying creatures of all time, were big enough to cast huge shadows over their ground-dwelling cousins.

▲ CLAMMING UP

With a 10-foot wingspan, *Dsungaripterus* (SUNG-ah-RIP-teh-rus) wasn't one of the largest flying reptiles, but it was still large compared to a human being. This Chinese reptile from the Cretaceous period had an interesting beak that experts believe was specially shaped for eating its favorite food: clams. It's thought that it used its beak to pry clams apart, and the flat teeth at the back of its beak could have broken up the shells.

▶ BIGGEST EVER?

The wingspan of Quetzalcoatlus, the biggest of the flying reptiles, was around 36 feet across—the same as that of a four-seater light aircraft! It wasn't until American scientist Paul MacCready built a full-size remote-controlled model in 1984 that scientists discovered how Quetzalcoatlus flew. The model clearly proved that Quetzalcoatlus flapped its wings like a bird— rather than gliding. MacCready's model went on to star in movies and on television.

LIGHTWEIGHT ▶

Ornithocheirus (or-NITH-oh-KEE-rus) had a giant wingspan to rival Quetzalcoatlus. Like its giant relation, Ornithocheirus was also very light. Paleontologists believe it may well have weighed less than 220 pounds, about the same as an adult human. This lack of weight was not the result of dieting, but because of its hollow bones—which were both strong and very light. Without these featherweight bones, there is no way that Ornithocheirus could have got off the ground.

Pterosaurs often had striking, elaborate crests on their heads.

◀ BAT BIRD

Like many of the flying reptiles, *Pteranodon* (teh-RAN-oh-don) looked like a cross between a lizard, a bird, and a bat. It used its huge beak to scoop fish out of the water, and the crest on its head may have been used to help it steer, a bit like the tail fin on an airplane. Its wings looked bat-like, with a leathery skin attaching the front and back legs. Unlike bats, Pteranodon did not hang upside down in caves, but probably nested on cliffs like seabirds do today.

SEA MONSTERS

During the Mesozoic era, giant animals could be found everywhere—including in the oceans. The sea was packed with enormous carnivores gliding through the water, constantly on the lookout for their next meal.

OVERINFLATED ▶

At around 80 feet in length, *Liopleurodon* (LEE-oh-PLORE-oh-don) has for many years had the reputation of being one of the record-breakers of the seas. However, more recent estimates put Liopleurodon closer to 33–49 feet. Very few remains have been discovered, so figuring out its size is difficult. What we do know is that it was a ferocious predator with a huge skull around 10 feet long, full of sharp teeth.

▶ PLIOSAUR PREDATOR

Kronosaurus was a Pliosaur, a species of short-necked marine reptile who terrorized the oceans of the Mesozoic era. Like modern-day sharks, Kronosaurus regarded anything that crossed its path as potential lunch. Around 40 feet long, with four strong flippers, Kronosaurus probably swam like a turtle—a massive, ferocious, meat-eating turtle, obviously!

LONG-NECKED LUNCH ▶

Plesiosaurs were a species of long-necked marine reptile, and *Elasmosaurus* (ee-LAZ-moh-SORE-us) took this to the extreme. It may well have been as long as 46 feet but half of its length was made up of its neck. Although Elasmosaurus was huge, it had a relatively small head, but it was big enough for catching and eating its favorite prey of fish and squid.

The first Plesiosaur remains were discovered in England in the early 1800s.

▼ CROC SHOCK

Did you know that some prehistoric creatures are still with us today? Although modern crocodiles can grow up to a huge 23 feet in length, this achievement pales into insignificance when they are compared to their ancient relatives. *Sarcosuchus* (sar-co-SOOK-us) was a river-dwelling monster of the Cretaceous period who grew to over 40 feet long. At this size it was big enough to prey not only on fish, but also on any unsuspecting dinosaurs that came for a drink at the wrong time.

SIMPLY HUGE!

As we have seen, the Mesozoic era was a time of extremes, with the largest animals ever to walk the planet existing at this time. But even among these massive monsters some creatures stood head and shoulders above the rest. Let's look at the record breakers.

MIGHTY MEAT-MUNCHER ▶

Now considered the biggest of the carnivorous dinosaurs, *Spinosaurus* (spin-oh-SORE-us) was a huge 56 feet in length. This North African predator also had a huge sail on its back, which some experts believe may have helped to regulate the dinosaur's temperature in a similar way to Stegosaurus's plates. Despite being the largest carnivore ever discovered, this massive meat-eater didn't chase other dinosaurs for its lunch—its favorite food was fish.

◀ HITTING THE HEIGHTS

Brachiosaurus has held the record for being the tallest dinosaur for many years now. At around 50 feet tall, this lumbering reptile could reach the leaves of even the tallest trees. This meant it could nibble on some of the tastiest foliage while other, shorter sauropods had to forage at lower levels. However, new discoveries from South America might knock this Jurassic giant from its perch. But until paleontologists find more evidence, Brachiosaurus is still number one.

LONG STRETCH ▶

The record for the longest dinosaur ever discovered goes to Seismosaurus. This relative of Diplodocus could grow to an estimated 115 feet, with its huge neck making up much of its length. Its tail would have made a fearsome weapon when being used like a whip to ward off potential attackers. It's also possible that Seismosaurus may have been able to raise itself up on its back legs to scare off predators—after all, no one would fancy getting stamped on by one of those big feet!

Some people believe that Seismosaurus is actually Diplodocus and not a separate species at all.

▼ HEAVYWEIGHT GIANT

Very few remains have been found of the South American sauropod *Argentinosaurus* (ar-jen-TEEN-o-SORE-us). Despite this, paleontologists know it was big—very big. They calculate that its weight was between 55 and 110 tons, making it the heaviest dinosaur yet discovered. It's a bit more difficult to estimate what its length may have been, but potentially it may well have been the longest and tallest dinosaur ever.

PREHISTORIC WORLD

THE FIRST DAYS

If you had the chance to see the world as it was about 4.5 billion years ago, when it first came into being, you would find that it did not look the way it does today. Back then, it was little more than a ball of molten rock. Eventually the planet cooled, rains fell, and seas formed, but the Earth was surrounded by poisonous gases—not an enticing prospect!

SIGNS OF LIFE

The first living things on Earth were not impressive to look at. In fact they were microscopic bacteria, so your chances of seeing them with the naked eye would have been zero. The bacteria and microbes that first appeared on Earth produced oxygen, the gas most life needs to breathe. Some bacteria formed colonies which, over time, became stromatolites (a type of layered fossil). Some stromatolites are over three billion years old!

You can still see stromatolites today. Hamelin Pool in western Australia is a famous site where these ancient structures can be found.

◄ WATERY WONDERS

The early oceans were the place to be if you were looking for life. After bacteria came simple animals such as sponges and jellyfish. However, some of the earliest life-forms were the trilobites. Looking bit like marine wood lice, they were an early success story—the resemblance isn't really surprising, as they're related. Trilobites ruled the oceans for nearly 300 million years despite the fact that the biggest of them only measured around 30 inches. However, all good things must come to an end and trilobites vanished from the seas about 250 million years ago.

▶ NOT SO FUNNY

The earliest predators were a strange-looking bunch. Take *Anomalocaris* (a-nom-uh-lo-CARE-is), for example—it was the scourge of the seas over 500 million years ago. It looked like a large shrimp with trunklike arms next to its mouth for catching prey. Or there's *Eurypterids* (you-RIP-ter-ids), which looked like a bug-eyed monster. These creatures might have looked odd, but they were good at one thing in particular, catching prey; and when you're a predator, that's all that counts.

▼ LATE DEVELOPER

The first fish made an appearance over 500 million years ago, but they were quite small and their mouths were always open as they didn't have jaws! Things developed over the next 100 million years and, by then, *Dunkleosteus* (dunk-lee-OWE-stee-us), a chunky, 33-foot-long super-predator, terrorized the seas. Around this time the first sharks appeared, so the ocean was a dangerous place for any lunch-sized creatures.

ON THE LAND

The survival instinct is one reason why animals evolve. In the beginning, most animals lived in the sea. To escape all those ocean predators, some species crawled onto dry land and started living there.

IT'S A MYSTERY

Scientists aren't sure exactly what the first animal to venture onto land was. We do know that it must have been able to breathe both on land and underwater. Scientists think that fish developed the ability to take breaths of air, and then began to pull themselves out of the water. Some experts believe an animal called *Pederpes* (peh-DER-pees) was the first creature to walk on the land. It lived around 350 million years ago and there have been creatures living on land ever since.

▼ PLANTS POP UP

The first plants appeared over 400 million years ago. They were hugely important, as they changed the makeup of the atmosphere. One of the most widely known is *Cooksonia*. It was small and insignificant and didn't have any leaves or flowers, but it was a start. Over the next few million years, plants evolved from these humble origins and some grew into huge forests.

BIG INSECTS ▶

Once the land was conquered, the air came next. Insects were the first creatures to become airborne, though it took them a while—about 70 million years to be exact—as the first insects couldn't fly. Once they had evolved, around 330 million years ago, they made up for lost time. Some of the most impressive insects ever seen appeared—for example, dragonflies with wingspans 28 inches across!

An animal that can breathe both on land and in water is called an amphibian.

▼ FINTASTIC

Around 70 million years after animals first left the water, the reptiles evolved. Originally they were quite small but soon developed into more formidable creatures. One of the most ferocious was *Dimetrodon* (di-MET-ro-don), who stalked the Earth around 270 million years ago. One of its more noticeable features was the bony fin on its back. Scientists think this might have helped Dimetrodon to warm up. As a reptile it would have been cold-blooded, and so would have relied on the warmth of the sun to generate body heat. Dimetrodon might have looked pretty awesome, but compared to the reptiles that appeared a few million years later, it was nothing!

DINO WORLD

It's hard to imagine a world in which the only living creatures were reptiles, especially ones that came in such a huge variety of shapes and sizes! However, such was the reign of the dinosaurs in the prehistoric era…

▼ SNACK ATTACK

If you were a small dinosaur, the last thing you wanted to encounter was a much larger dino on the lookout for a tasty morsel. However, it is estimated that only 35 percent of dinosaurs were carnivores, while the remaining 65 percent were happy to be herbivores.

◀ BIGGEST OF ALL?

We all know that some dinosaurs were big, but we're not sure exactly which one was the biggest of all. Current favorites to take the record include Argentinosaurus and Seismosaurus. At lengths of up to 115 feet and weighing in at over 66 tons, these giants could peer over the top of a house—and leave some enormous footprints in your flower beds!

A new dinosaur species was discovered in February 2011. Nicknamed "Thunder-thighs," Brontomerus mcintoshi had huge thigh muscles.

▲ WINGED WONDERS

Dinosaurs were not the only reptiles to roam the Earth at this time. There were others too, such as the flying Pterosaurs. They had leathery wings, a bit like a bat's, and could, scientists believe, glide and soar through the air. The largest was Quetzalcoatlus, with a wingspan of around 40 feet, but not all pterosaurs were this big—some were no bigger than a small bird.

SMALL AND FEATHERY

Not all dinosaurs were earth-shaking giants. Many were small, scurrying creatures no bigger than chickens. It's hard to say which dinosaur was the smallest—so little evidence remains of some species—and it is difficult to tell whether they are adults or just young dinosaurs. Many believe that small dinosaurs, such as *Caudipteryx* (caw-DIP-ter-iks), were covered in feathers to help keep them warm.

NEW ARRIVALS

No one is sure why dinosaurs completely disappeared all those years ago, but we do know that 50 percent of all life was wiped out. This was bad news for the dinosaurs—but it worked out well for the mammals.

A WHAT?

A mammal is warm-blooded, which means it generates its own body heat—unlike a reptile—and gives birth to live young. The first mammals shared the planet with the dinosaurs. In those days, many mammals were quite small, about the size of a rat. However, recent finds suggest that some mammals grew a bit bigger—to over 3 feet in fact—and some even ate small dinosaurs!

MONKEYING AROUND ▶

When the dinosaurs died out, the lack of competition gave the mammals room to grow and diversify. Around sixty million years ago the first primates—apes and monkeys—evolved. The most complete remains found so far belong to *Proconsul africanus* (pro-CON-sul afri-KHAN-us), which lived around eighteen million years ago. It walked on four legs and probably ate fruit. I wonder if there were bananas back then?

GIDDY UP ▶

The first horses appeared over forty million years ago. One of the most famous is *Hyracotherium* (high-rah-co-THEER-ium), often called *Eohippus* (ee-oh-HIP-us) or the "dawn horse." It didn't look much like a horse; for a start, it had toes instead of hooves, much like a dog. The differences don't end there; Hyracotherium was only 8 inches high. It's safe to say you wouldn't be jumping many fences if you rode one of those!

There is a third type of mammal, known as monotremes—these are mammals that lay eggs!

◀ MARSUPIALS

Marsupials are mammals that carry their newborn young in a pouch, where they continue to develop, such as kangaroos. In the past marsupials were much more common than they are now. The first marsupials rubbed shoulders with the dinosaurs and later evolved into all shapes and sizes. Some were carnivores, too, such as *Sparassodonta patene* (spar-ASS-oh-don-ta pah-ten), a fox-sized predator from Brazil. No doubt it was a bit fiercer than a koala!

75

OCEAN LIFE

While the dinosaurs appeared and then disappeared on the land, below the waves there was a lot going on, too. Life in the underwater world was constantly expanding and diversifying, producing a vast range of strange and fascinating creatures.

▼ SHELL-SHOCK

Turtles have been around for over 100 million years and, long ago, some of them were huge. *Archelon* (ARK-eh-lon) lived alongside the dinosaurs and died out at the same time. Apart from its size—it was about as big as a car—it was different in other ways from today's turtles. For example, its shell wasn't hard but leathery—leaving it vulnerable to attack. There's not much point in having a shell if it's soft, is there?

◄ BIG FISH

At just under 100 feet long, *Leedsichthys* (leeds-ICK-thees) was not only the biggest fish of its time, it was the biggest fish of all time. It may seem odd, but Leedsichthys wasn't a mean old predator; this huge fish ate tiny sea creatures called plankton, which was good news for all the other fish!

▲ BIG SNAPPER

A lot of the animals we know today had relatives that lived millions of years ago. This is true of crocodiles, whose ancestors not only knew dinosaurs, but possibly ate them, too. Sarcosuchus, which lived over 100 million years ago, was certainly big enough to snap up an unwary dinosaur. It was around 40 feet long and had jaws big enough to swallow your teacher whole!

Leedsichthys was alive at the same time as the dinosaurs. It was swimming in the seas around 160 million years ago.

◄ BACK TO THE SEA

After waiting for so long for creatures to come out of the water and onto the land, it seems odd that some did the reverse—but that's exactly what whales did. They evolved from land mammals that began to spend increasing amounts of time in the water, until eventually their legs turned into flippers. The first creature to look like a modern whale was *Basilosaurus* (bah-sil-oh-SAW-rus), who lived around 45 million years ago. If it had been able to foresee the problems its descendants encounter today, it might have stayed on land!

EVOLUTION

On land, the mammals faced no great competition and, like the dinosaurs before them, they grew and evolved into a range of species in different colors, shapes, and sizes.

▼ MONSTER MAMMAL

If you think mammals such as elephants are big, you haven't seen anything yet! The *Indricotherium* (IN-drik-oh-theer-ium) was the biggest mammal ever to walk the Earth. It lived over 25 million years ago and was around 13 feet tall. Fortunately for everything else that lived at the time, Indricotherium ate plants, not meat. In fact Indricotherium is a distant relative of today's rhinoceros. Do you think it would have been as grumpy and shortsighted as today's rhinos?

DANGEROUS GROUND ▶

Today we think of sloths as slow-moving creatures who spend most of their lives asleep in the trees. However, once there were sloths who lived on the ground, and some of them were huge!

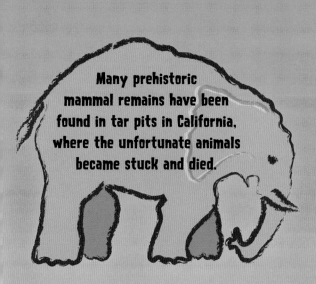

Many prehistoric mammal remains have been found in tar pits in California, where the unfortunate animals became stuck and died.

▶ SURPRISINGLY SMALL

Not all the ancient mammals were giants, of course; some of them were smaller versions of animals we know today. For example, there was a species of dwarf elephant who lived as recently as around 8,000 years ago. These elephants often lived on islands and some were less than 3 feet tall.

Despite their size, they still had relatively large ears, a trunk, and tusks.

▶ BAD KITTY

There were some pretty mean mammalian carnivores around, and like today some of the most impressive were catlike. *Thylacosmilus* (thy-la-COS-mih-lus) was a marsupial who lived in South America and it was about the size of a jaguar. Its two huge fangs were its most striking feature. It's safe to say that this was one cat you wouldn't want as a pet but, amazingly, this fearsome character was outdone by even bigger and meaner saber-toothed cats.

EARLY MAN

T he story of human history is mightily confused. For a start, there's no clear picture of exactly how we developed. However, we do know that there were many different types of early human, all of whom died out apart from our own particular species. Meet the ancestors!

▼ HE OR SHE?

The oldest human remains ever found came from Africa and are nearly six million years old. Back then, humans resembled apes and spent a lot of their time in trees. One of the most famous discoveries is *Australopithecus afarensis* (OS-trah-lop-ITH-ee-cus aff-ah-REN-sis). The remains were nicknamed "Lucy," as they were thought to be the bones of a female. However, some scientists think "she" might have actually been a "he." Girl or boy, Lucy is over three million years old and stood about 3 feet high.

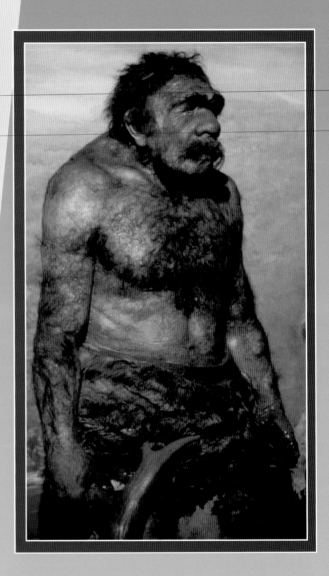

▲ FAMILY FEUD

There was another highly successful species of human around—the Neanderthals. Shorter and heavier than *Homo sapiens* (HOE-mo SAY-pee-uns), they had been living for much longer—from around 150,000 years earlier. Neanderthals were thought to be more primitive than Homo sapiens. However, some scientists now believe that they too were capable of being artists as well as hunters. Whatever the truth, the Neanderthals finally disappeared around 30,000 years ago, outperformed by their cousins, the Homo sapiens.

CAVE ARTISTS ▶

Our own direct relatives—Homo sapiens—have been around for at least 130,000 years. What made us different was our ability to think. Being a bit brainier meant that Homo sapiens were able to plan and work well together. This left time for indulging in such exciting pastimes as cave art—it would be a long time before we invented television! Being clever also made us adaptable; and if you can adapt you can survive—and that's just what we did.

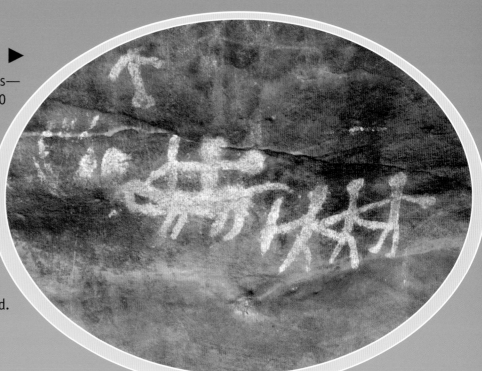

Our human ancestors and near relatives are known as "hominids."

▼ NO-BRAINER

Recently a small skeleton was found on the Indonesian island of Flores. About 12,000 years old, the skeleton appeared to have a smaller brain than Homo sapiens. About 3 feet tall, it was nicknamed the Flores Hobbit. Scientists thought they had found a new species of human being. Now, however, many believe that it is the remains of a small Homo sapiens with a disease that made its brain smaller. It just goes to show how difficult studying the past can be.

ICE AGE

FROZEN IN TIME

An ice age is when the world's temperature drops and stays low for a long period of time and ice spreads out from the poles. Throughout history there have been lots of ice ages. But when people talk about the Ice Age they mean the one that began around 2.5 million years ago and lasted until about 10,000 years ago.

▲ MAKE UP YOUR MIND

When people think of the Ice Age they think of snow, cold weather, and strange shaggy beasts. It's true that, at times, great sheets of ice covered a lot of the Earth's surface; however, this is only part of the story. At other times the climate was quite mild. The ice sheets retreated north and the temperature rose before things started to cool down once again.

◀ WHAT CAUSED THE ICE AGE?

The Earth gets its warmth from the Sun. Any slight variation in the Earth's orbit—the path it takes as it goes round the Sun—can lead to big variations in temperature. Sometimes the Earth leans slightly closer to or farther away from the Sun, which can result in the Earth heating up or cooling down a bit. During the last Ice Age, the Earth's Northern Hemisphere was probably tilted a little farther away than normal and the result was that things got a little bit chilly.

WHERE DID THEY GO? ▶

The end of the Ice Age was remarkable on two fronts: firstly, it got a lot warmer; secondly, a lot of animals became extinct. No one is sure exactly why. Perhaps they were hunted to extinction? Perhaps they didn't like the warmer weather? Perhaps the vegetation changed too much? In short, we just don't know.

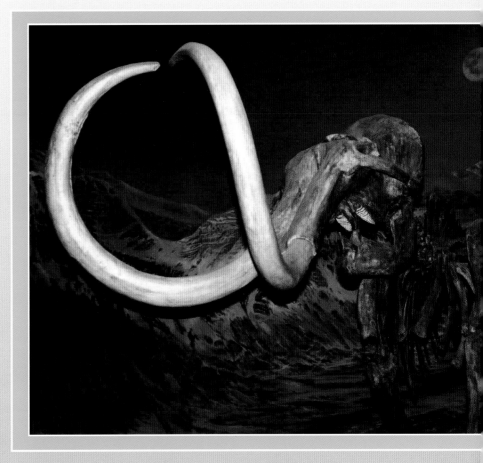

Some scientists believe that we are still in the Ice Age but it doesn't feel cold because we're in one of the warmer periods.

HERE COME THE HUMANS ▶

Another notable feature of the Ice Age was the story of the humans. In the Northern Hemisphere, a species called *Homo heidelbergensis* (HOE-mo hi-del-burg-EN-sis) arrived first. They did well until the arrival of the Neanderthals, who in turn flourished until our direct ancestors the Homo sapiens turned up. Why did the humans survive when lots of other animals didn't? Well, we had a lot going for us—we were adaptable, could work as a team, could fashion tools, and had language. And there's a good chance that we were responsible for killing everything else off!

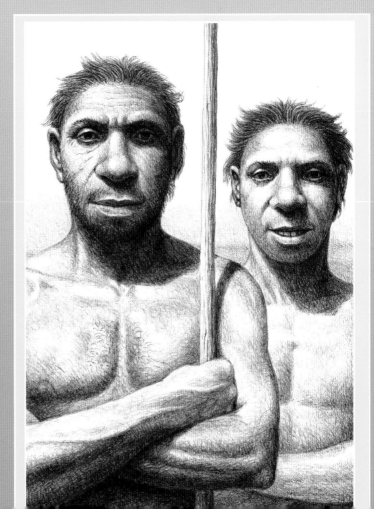

HAIRY BEASTS

I f you're out and about in the cold it's a good idea to wrap up warm. That's precisely what many animals did during the Ice Age. They grew thick shaggy coats to keep themselves from freezing to death.

▲ TINY EARS

The mastodon might look like a mammoth, but it's a different species entirely. It had straighter tusks and different teeth, which better suited its diet of tree leaves as opposed to grass. Like the mammoth, the mastodon had very small ears, which helped it to cut back on the amount of heat it lost from its body. After all, it makes sense not to leave anything out in the cold that doesn't need to be there.

◀ GRUMPY

A common sight across Europe was the woolly rhinoceros. This two-horned beast was a close relative of today's rare Sumatran rhinoceros. At around 12 feet long, the woolly rhino was pretty big, but it was nothing compared to *Elasmotherium* (ee-LAZ-moh-THERE-i-um)—another Ice Age rhino from Russia. This was almost twice the size of its woolly cousin and well known for being grumpy, so it would have been wise to stay clear of it!

◀ WELL ADAPTED

One hairy creature that was particularly well adapted to the freezing temperatures was the musk ox. Its shaggy coat was perfect for keeping the cold at bay. It was a survivor, too. Its direct relatives are still with us today—though they're not quite as big as their ancestors, which were nearly 2 feet taller.

Mammoths had a flap of skin that kept cold air from getting up their rears.

SNOWPLOW ▶

The one animal most people think of when you mention the Ice Age is the woolly mammoth. There were actually lots of different kinds of mammoth and not all of them were covered in shaggy fur, but they did all have huge, curved tusks. Scientists think that the mammoths used the tusks to push the snow away so they could get to the grass, which they ate. In a way, mammoths were like hairy snowplows.

MEAT-EATERS

A nimals have been eating other animals for as long as creatures have fancied a juicy steak rather than a bunch of leaves. That was true for the Ice Age, too, which produced a group of carnivores who were fairly similar to the meat-eaters we have today—only bigger.

▼ SMILEY

The most famous Ice Age carnivore was *Smilodon* (smile-oh-don)—the saber-toothed tiger. Smilodon wasn't actually related to today's tigers, but it was as large as the present-day big cats and much stockier. Those huge fangs look pretty fearsome and they were handy for puncturing the skin of their prey, but they were no use at crunching through bone. This meant that Smilodon had to leave most of the meat on its kills as it couldn't eat it without risking damage to its precious teeth. So no juicy ribs for these cats!

BALDY ▶

The largest lion to walk the planet terrorized plant-eaters and unsuspecting carnivores alike across Ice Age Europe. It was called the cave lion and at around 10 feet long it was considerably bigger than today's lions. Unlike modern lions, male cave lions didn't have manes—strange, as you'd think you'd need as much hair as possible in the cold.

SHORT AND LONG

The biggest meat-eater of the Ice Age was the short-faced bear. Its face may have been on the short side for a bear, but everything else about this prehistoric teddy was huge. When it stood on its hind legs it would have been around 10 feet tall—easily bigger than today's largest bear, the polar bear. But was this giant a killer? Some people suggest that the short-faced bear was actually a scavenger and that it may well have munched on berries too, like today's bears.

The biggest predator on land was a wolf-like animal called Andrewsarchus. It was more than 15 feet long!

◀ DIRE STRAITS

One common Ice Age predator was the dire wolf. These beasts were similar to their modern-day counterparts but were a bit larger. The good news for their prospective victims was that they had shorter legs than today's wolves, so they may not have been as good at getting about. The bad news was that they hunted in packs, so if you got away from one, there was always a chance another one would get you. More bad news—they had really big teeth, too!

SUPER-SIZED

A feature of the Ice Age period was that many of the animals were a great deal bigger than they are today. Any animal weighing more than 100 pounds is classed as megafauna, or a large animal. The Ice Age had plenty of megafauna—including many giant varieties of species we are still familiar with today. Ice Age Earth was certainly the land of the giants.

Glyptodon was a kind of armadillo that was as big as a small car!

▼ SUPER SLOTH

The biggest sloth of all time was *Megatherium* (meg-ah-THERE-ee-um)—it was around 20 feet long and weighed as much as an elephant. It was much too large to live in the trees, of course, so it lived on the ground. You might think this left it vulnerable to attack, but any predator who got too close would get a whack from those powerful arms and sharp claws.

BOING BOING! ▶

Megafauna could be found all over the world. Australia was home to giant kangaroos known as *Procoptodon* (pro-COP-toh-don). They stood around twice as tall as the present-day kangaroos but had a very short face compared to today's beasts. Not that you would want to make jokes about them—another notable difference was the large claw at the end of each foot!

GIANT LUMBERJACK

Animals that today we think of as being quite small often grew big during the Ice Age. Take the beaver, for example, which grew to the size of a bear. Imagine the size of tree that that toothy terror could have chomped its way through!

◀ IRISH GIANT

Today's male deer, or stags as they are called, grow antlers on their heads. The more impressive the antlers, the more likely the stags are to mate. However, even the most impressive of today's antlers would look a little feeble compared to those of *Megaloceros* (meg-a-LOSS-er-oss), sometimes known as the Irish elk. Their antlers could measure around 12 feet across, but this isn't really surprising as the deer itself was around 6 feet tall, making it the largest deer ever to have lived. Unfortunately it also seems to have been very tasty, as it was hunted to extinction around 7,500 years ago.

A MIXED BUNCH

As the climate during the Ice Age varied so much, the types of animals living in just one area also varied over time. As things grew hotter or colder, the species of animals changed, with some surprising outcomes.

▲ GETTING THE HUMP

You generally think of camels living somewhere very dry and dusty, but until around 11,000 years ago they lived in many areas of the United States! Remains that have been found suggest that this extinct version of the camel might have looked a bit like today's Bactrian camel—that's the one-humped variety to you and me. It might even have had no hump at all.

◀ DARK HORSE

For many years it was thought that horses were introduced to the United States by the Spanish after Christopher Columbus arrived in 1492. In a way this story is correct, as there were no horses on the continent at that time. However, horses had been living in America since before the Ice Age. Around 10,000 years ago they either died out or moved away, possibly due to the changing climate. The next horses to set foot on American soil were those that arrived by boat with the Spanish explorers.

JUST LIKE AFRICA ▶

If you see elephants wandering around and a hippopotamus in the river, you can be fairly sure you are in Africa. In the Ice Age, you might be in London! Over 120,000 years ago, elephants and hippos would have been an everyday sight across much of Britain, but it's safe to say you don't get many hippos in the Thames these days!

The United States had its own version of a cheetah. It was called Mirocynonyx and was probably the speediest predator around.

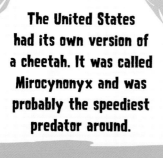

▼ TINY TUSKER

Although many Ice Age animals were bigger than their modern-day counterparts, not all were—some were smaller. There was a small version of mammoth that lived in what is now the Californian Channel Islands. It was just over 5 feet tall at the shoulder, which would make it shorter than many adult humans. This example of pygmy versions of animals isn't that rare either. It seems that sometimes animals adjust their size to their surroundings, so a small island is often home to small animals.

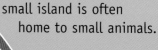

HUMANKIND

It's easy to think that our ancient ancestors were simple folk. The image of a caveman is someone who wears animal furs, carries a club, and grunts a lot. However, the people of the Ice Age were a lot more sophisticated than that and their ability to survive is proof of their intelligence.

▲ OBSOLETE OR MURDERED?

Neanderthals were one branch of the human family tree that was well-adapted to living in the Ice Age. They were short and stocky, which helped to keep them warm. It also turns out that, as well as being very strong, they were much more intelligent than scientists used to believe. However, about 28,000 years ago Neanderthals disappeared. It was believed that they were unable to adapt to warmer conditions, but new finds dispute this. It now seems likely that they were wiped out by competing Homo sapiens.

◀ AND THE WINNER IS...

The end of the Ice Age saw the arrival of our very own ancestors, Homo sapiens. Compared to the Neanderthals, our forbears were taller and slimmer, with longer limbs. This made them better suited to moving around the no-longer-frozen landscape. Also, Homo sapiens made finer tools and weapons than their Neanderthal cousins and would later develop farming techniques. It may well have been this all-around ability that has seen our version of humans hang about for so long.

VANDALS ▶

One activity that Ice Age people indulged in has been very helpful for scientists and historians today. Our ancestors decorated the walls of caves with their own artwork, often showing hunting scenes and pictures of animals. This gives us an idea of what life was like during the Ice Age. These paintings are very precious—which is not what people normally say when they see graffiti on walls!

Some scientists believe that modern humans are descended from as few as 10,000 ancient Homo sapiens!

▼ EXTERMINATE

It was long thought that our ancestors were responsible for killing off animals such as the mammoths. It's true that Ice Age people did hunt these beasts—favorite techniques included chasing them over cliffs or into specially dug pits—but they may not have been as destructive as we first thought. Some scientists now argue that the changing climate had more to do with the extinctions than people did.

THE EVIDENCE

Scientists and historians re-create what the past might have been like by looking at things that have survived from a particular time. Fortunately, there are plenty of Ice Age remains—skeletons, fossils, even tools, along with clues to the diet of people and animals—so we have lots of information to go on.

BACK FROM THE DEAD

Some mammoth remains are so well-preserved that it has led some scientists to believe they might be able to bring mammoths back from the dead. The idea would be to take cells from the mammoths and cross them with cells from the mammoth's closest living relative, the Indian elephant. Theoretically it's possible, but in practice it's a very difficult proposition—and no one knows if it would work or even if it's a good idea!

Scientists know what mammoths ate because they have found the remains of food in the stomachs of mammoths frozen in the tundra.

◀ STICKY END

Asphalt is a naturally occurring sticky substance, a bit like tar. At Rancho La Brea in Los Angeles, great pools of asphalt have been trapping animals for hundreds of thousands of years. It's an unfortunate way for the poor creatures to die but it means that their bones don't erode or get dispersed. As a result, the fossils found in La Brea are of an excellent quality. What's more, there are thousands of them—including wolves, mammoths, and Smilodons!

PERFECTLY PRESERVED

Imagine going for a walk and bumping into a mammoth. Well, that's exactly what might happen if you were wandering around the frozen Russian tundra. The mammoths found there aren't alive, of course, but some are almost perfectly preserved. The one big advantage of the cold tundra is that it preserves things—just like a freezer. The only difference is that it's unlikely you're going to find Ice Age beasts in your freezer!

► PLANTING EVIDENCE

Across Europe and the United States there are caves where both people and animals have lived. These caves often provide invaluable information on what life was like, as they not only contain bones—often the remains of meals—but also samples of pollen. The pollen tells us what kind of plants were growing at different times, which in turn gives us an idea of how warm or cold the weather was.

REPTILES

A BIG FAMILY

What do you think of when you hear the word "reptile"? Many people think of cold, slimy snakes, but they couldn't be more wrong. True, snakes are reptiles, but they are nothing like you might imagine, and they are just one member of the extended reptile family. There are over seven thousand types of reptile and they come in lots of shapes and sizes, from tiny lizards to huge tortoises.

MEET THE ANCESTORS ▶

Even the biggest of today's lizards don't match up to their huge predecessors, the dinosaurs. So the next time a snake gives you the shivers or a turtle gives you a fright, be thankful it isn't a T. rex. In fact, reptiles were around long before the dinosaurs appeared. The oldest fossil reptile found so far is over 340 million years old.

BIG AND SMALL ▼

Even though today's reptiles aren't as big as they were thousands of years ago, they still vary greatly in size. Anacondas—giant South American snakes—can grow to between 26 and 36 feet in length—that's about the length of two large family cars. At the other end of the scale, the smallest reptiles are geckos. Some don't grow any longer than around 1 inch.

People who study reptiles are called herpetologists.

SUN LOVERS ▶

Reptiles can be found virtually anywhere, whether it's in a city like Los Angeles, a desert in Africa, or even in the depths of the Indian Ocean. But you'll not find one in most Arctic areas or in Antarctica. That's due to the fact that reptiles don't like the cold, so you'll never bump into one on a ski slope!

BODY PARTS

So, what makes a reptile? Although they may look very different from each other, all reptiles have several characteristics in common—even though they may appear very different at first sight.

▼ NOT GOOD IN THE MORNING

Reptiles are often called cold-blooded, which means they can't generate their own body heat. Instead, reptiles have to rely on the sun to warm them up. Reptiles are very sluggish when they are cold, which makes it easy for predators to catch them. The warmer the atmosphere, the quicker reptiles warm up, which is why they don't live in cold regions.

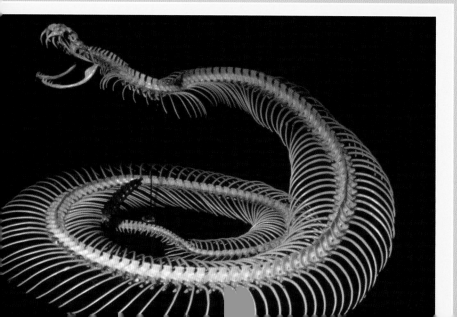

◄ BITS AND PIECES

All reptiles have a skeleton with a backbone and they lay eggs, which have a waterproof shell. Remarkably, all reptiles either have four legs or had ancestors with four legs—this includes snakes. Of course, snakes lost their legs a long time ago, but you can still see small traces of legs on some snakes' skeletons.

SCALES ▼

All reptiles have scales, which are made from keratin—the same stuff your fingernails are made from. Reptiles' skin is also very dry as it is specially designed to keep them from losing water from their bodies. On some reptiles, such as crocodiles, the scales fuse together to form plates, which makes the skin tougher.

Reptiles can virtually shut their bodies down if they get too cold.

GOING UP ▶

Reptiles are great climbers and this is due to their special feet. Reptiles have clawed feet, which are an obvious help. But some lizards, such as geckos, have millions of little hairs, called setae, on the bottom of their feet. These tiny hairs allow geckos to climb walls with the greatest of ease.

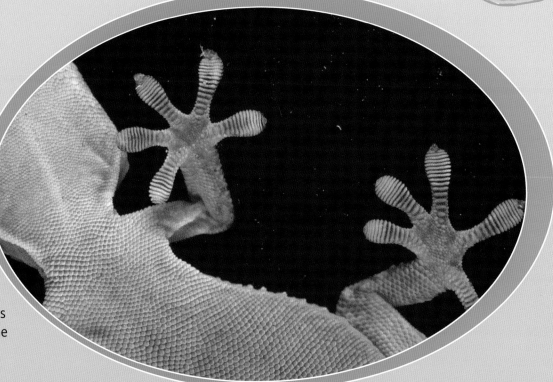

THE BIG BOYS

The first fossils to be found were thought to be the bones of monsters or dragons. Explorers and traders who traveled to different countries would return with tales of fearsome-looking reptiles and even taller tales of gigantic beasts. These modern-day "monsters" may not be gigantic, but they are still impressive creatures.

It was once believed that a stare from a basilisk lizard was enough to kill you!

◀ WORTH MONITORING

The heavyweights of the lizard world are the monitors, and king among them is the Komodo dragon. Found only on the island of Komodo and some neighboring islands in Indonesia, these fearsome creatures grow to over 10 feet in length and weigh more than two people put together. They are big enough to kill and eat deer and have even been known to eat children!

▼ PROUD PARENTS

A crocodile might be the last thing you want to see when you go for a swim, but they make great parents. Crocodiles are one of the few members of the reptile family who take care of their young. They make nests for their eggs and, when they hatch, the crocodile is there to take care of its new brood. Some species even carry their babies from the nest to the water in their mouth—and aren't tempted to eat a single one!

▲ SNEAKY SNAPPER

There are over twenty species of crocodilian, including crocodiles, alligators, and caimans. The biggest are saltwater crocodiles, which can grow to more than 20 feet long and weigh more than a car. Crocodilians are good at hiding in water to ambush their prey. They sneak up on animals who come to the water to drink, then lunge out at them quickly. Some species can even jump straight out of the water to seize their prey.

NOT A PRETTY SIGHT ▶

The marine iguana is so odd-looking that even the renowned naturalist Charles Darwin described them as "disgusting." However, he was probably impressed by their swimming skills, as this strange lizard can stay underwater for up to an hour.

SHY SNAKES

Right at the top of the list of things that people are scared of are snakes, but many people with a snake phobia have never seen one. In fact, snakes are very shy animals and are much happier scurrying away from people than attacking them. Many snakes are harmless anyway, and even the most poisonous ones will only bite if provoked or surprised.

▼ FANG-TASTIC

Poisonous snakes don't have the biggest fangs you're likely to see in the animal kingdom, but they're very effective at what they do. Like hypodermic needles, snakes' fangs are perfect for injecting poison into their prey.

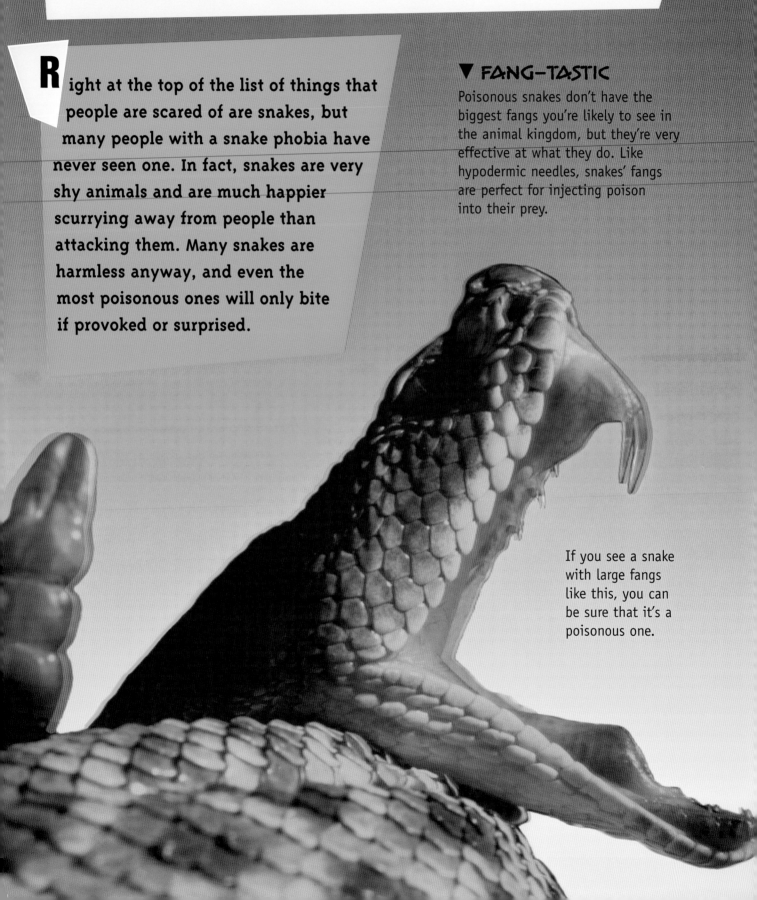

If you see a snake with large fangs like this, you can be sure that it's a poisonous one.

HOODED KING ▶

The most famous venomous snake is the cobra with its distinctive hood of skin behind its head. The largest of the cobra family is the king cobra, which is so venomous that it can kill an elephant with a single bite.

▲ BIG SQUEEZE

The biggest snakes of all—the boas and pythons—are not venomous. They don't need to be—squeezing their victims really tightly in their coils is enough to kill them.

▼ GULP!

Snakes have very flexible jaws. When it comes to meal times, they open their mouths as wide as possible and swallow their prey whole—always headfirst, as it's easier to swallow that way.

Over 7,000 people are bitten by snakes in the United States every year. Luckily, very few cases prove fatal.

HARD SHELL

You might know them as slow-moving lettuce chompers, and it's true that often tortoises and turtles don't seem in much of a hurry. In spite of this, the chelonian family includes some truly remarkable animals. Some species travel thousands of miles across the oceans, others can live longer than practically any other animal on Earth. Take a peek under the shell of the chelonians and meet the truly terrific tortoises and turtles.

▲ HARD CASE

All members of the chelonian family have a shell. The shell is part of the turtle's skeleton and is generally very hard and protective. Some chelonians can even bring their legs, head, and tail into the shell for extra protection. But not all chelonian shells are hard. The leatherback turtle, for example, has a soft shell. This is because the leatherback swims to great depths in the ocean, where the water pressure would otherwise crack the shell.

WHAT'S WHAT? ▶

All chelonians are turtles, but the different types of turtle each have their own name. As a general rule of thumb, a tortoise lives on land and a turtle lives in the water.

FANTASTIC FLIPPERS ▼

There are over 250 species of turtle and tortoise, and many of them spend their time in water. Only seven species of turtle spend all their time in the ocean. These sea turtles, like this loggerhead turtle, have large flippers instead of legs and only come on land to lay their eggs.

▲ UNDER THREAT

Like many members of the reptile family, turtles are under threat. Loss of habitat, hunting, poaching, and pollution are slowly killing off some species of these ancient, stately creatures. In some countries, it is now illegal to have a tortoise as a pet unless it has been born in that country.

GENTLE GIANTS ▶

Some of the most famous tortoises of all are those found on the Galapagos Islands of the Pacific Ocean. These giants can measure over 3 feet from head to tail and weigh more than 440 pounds. Even more remarkably, these gentle giants can live for between 150 and 200 years.

PARTY TRICKS

With so many different types of reptile, it should come as no surprise that some of them look a little odd. And sometimes their behavior is strange, too!

▼ WALKING ON WATER

If a basilisk lizard is in a hurry and there's water in its path, the lizard won't go around it or swim across it. Instead, it picks up speed and runs over the top of it on two legs. This miraculous behavior has earned it the nickname the "Jesus lizard."

▲ BUG-EYED MARVEL

The chameleon is a remarkable beast. Not only does it have popping-out eyes that can move in opposite directions to each other and a long tongue that it can shoot out to catch flies, it can also change color. It is often thought chameleons change color to blend in with their surroundings, but some scientists believe the color change happens to show that a chameleon is angry or feels threatened.

Some lizards' tails snap off if they're captured, so they can escape.

▶ TREE HOPPER

You can find reptiles everywhere—under the ground, up trees, on the water, in the water, and even in the air. Some tree-dwelling lizards have taken to springing into the air to reach trees that are too far away. Although called flying dragons, these reptiles in fact use special flaps of skin to help them glide, like a hang glider, from tree to tree.

PUTTING ON A SHOW ▶

If reptiles feel threatened, the first thing they do is try to get away. If reptiles are cornered, however, they have different ways of reacting. Some reptiles will play dead, rattlesnakes will shake the tip of their tails to produce a rattling noise as a warning, but one of the most startling of displays comes from the frilled lizard of Australia. This lizard spreads out a frill around its head and hisses at the animal chasing it. The frill makes the lizard look much bigger than it is and, hopefully, puts off the attacker.

Contributor credits:
3-D glasses illustrator: Ian Thompson
3-D images: Pinsharp 3-D Graphics

Further credits by chapter:

DINOSAURS: THE BASICS
Author: Heather Amery
Picture credits: Ardea London Ltd; Discovery Communications
Inc; Natural History Museum (London); Oxford Scientific
(OSF)/Photolibrary.com; Science Photo Library.

DINOSAURS: THE FACTS
Author: Paul Harrison
Picture credits: Corbis; Getty Images; NHPA; Science Photo
Library.

T. REX
Author: Paul Harrison
Picture credits: Ardea London Ltd; Field Museum, Chicago;
Natural History Museum Picture Library (London); Nature
Picture Library; Oxford Scientific (OSF)/Photolibrary.com;
Science Photo Library.

GIANT DINOSAURS
Author: Paul Harrison
Picture credits: Bill Stoneham; Corbis; Getty Images; Jon
Hughes/pixelshack.com; Natural History Museum; Photoshot;
Reuters; Science Photo Library.

PREHISTORIC WORLD
Author: Paul Harrison
Picture credits: Corbis; Getty Images; Science Photo Library.

ICE AGE
Author: Paul Harrison
Picture credits: AKG; Corbis; FLPA; Getty Images; Indiana
State Museum and Historic Sites; Rex Features; Science Photo
Library; Shropshire County Museum Service; TopFoto.

REPTILES
Author: Paul Harrison
Picture credits: Nature Picture Library; NHPA; Oxford
Scientific (OSF)/Photolibrary.com; Science Photo Library;
John White Photos.

page 112: Getty Images